For _Steven Searcy_

"*The LORD bless you and keep you;
the LORD make his face shine upon you
and be gracious to you;
the LORD turn his face toward you
and give you peace*"

Numbers 6:24–26

From _The Stones_

Date _May 2005_

Congratulations!

Bright Hope for Your Future
Copyright 1998 by ZondervanPublishingHouse
ISBN 0310977487

Requests for information should be addressed to:
    Inspirio, the Gift Group of Zondervan
    Grand Rapids, Michigan 49530

Senior Editor: Gwen Ellis
Compiled by: Heidi S. Hess
Designed by: Mark Veldheer

Printed in China

00 01 02 03 /❖ HK/ 9 8 7 6 5 4

Bright Hope
for
Your Future

Compiled by Heidi S. Hess

inspirio

The gift group of Zondervan

If you are going to be used by God,
he is going to take you
through a number of experiences
that were not meant for you at all.
They are meant to make you
useful in his hands.

OSWALD CHAMBERS

Table of Contents

PART FOUR: Accept God's Good Gifts

PART FIVE: Seize the Day

PART ONE

Believe God Has a Great Future for You

"For I know the plans I have for you,"
declares the LORD,
"plans to prosper you and not to harm you,
plans to give you hope and a future."

JEREMIAH 29:11

When All Else Fails ... Trust and Believe

God's faithfulness is a steady source of comfort and strength in the highs and lows of life.

Hope in God is as unshakable as a rock. It means absolute assurance. It implies utter confidence in God's impeccable character. It denotes composed stability and strength in any situation no matter how drastic. It is overwhelming optimism in the darkest hour.

All of this energy is grounded in the eternal goodness of God Himself. It flows to us from the impeccable character of Christ. It stands sure in the power and person of His Wholesome Spirit....

God calls us to live our lives in a different dimension from that of the world around us. He quietly invites us to find our hope in Him. He urges us to plunge into the inner stream of His life, there to find the help and wholeness we need amid our distress. Our hope should be in God, not in man.

Phillip Keller

It is an equal failing to trust everybody, and to trust nobody.

English Proverb

The abdication of Belief
Makes the Behavior small—
Better an ignis fatuus
Than no illume at all.

Emily Dickinson

Know that the LORD is God. It is he who made us, and we are his;
we are his people, the sheep of his pasture. . . . For the LORD is
good and his love endures forever.

Psalm 100:3,5

I know whom I have believed, and am convinced that he is able to
guard what I have entrusted to him for that day.

2 Timothy 1:12

Dear friends, if our hearts do not condemn us, we have confidence
before God and receive from him anything we ask, because we
obey his commands and do what pleases him. And this is his
command: to believe in the name of his Son, Jesus Christ, and to
love one another as he commanded us.

1 John 3:21–23

In God We Have a Future and Hope

*By embracing the future with hope and perfect love, we can
be all that God intends us to be.*

We were made for God. Only in being in some respect like
Him, only by being a manifestation of His beauty,
lovingkindness, wisdom or goodness, has any earthly Beloved
excited our love.

It is not that we have loved them too much, but that we did
not quite understand what we were loving.

It is not that we shall be asked to turn from them, so dearly
familiar, to a Stranger.

When we see the face of God we shall know that we have
always known it. He has been a party to, has made, sustained
and moved moment by moment within, all our earthly experiences of innocent love. All that was true love in them was, even
on earth, far more His than ours, and ours only because His.

C. S. Lewis

When you say that a situation or a person is hopeless,
you are slamming the door in the face of God.

Charles L. Allen

Do not let your heart envy sinners,
    but always be zealous for the fear of the LORD.
There is surely a future hope for you,
    and your hope will not be cut off.
Listen, my son, and be wise,
    and keep your heart on the right path.
Do not join those who drink too much wine
    or gorge themselves on meat,
for drunkards and gluttons become poor,
    and drowsiness clothes them in rags.
Listen to your father, who gave you life,
    and do not despise your mother when she is old.
Buy the truth and do not sell it;
    get wisdom, discipline and understanding.
The father of a righteous man has great joy;
    he who has a wise son delights in him.

Proverbs 23:17–24

Are You Eager for Heaven?

When you were in school, you could hardly wait for exams to be over and summer vacation to begin. Now you're getting your wish … time for bigger and better things! And yet, no matter what you have in store for your future, these experiences are really just a "practice run" before the glories of heaven. Think about it: Would you live differently today if you knew that you were about to take your "final exams"?

I don't want God to be ashamed of me. I don't want him to blush when I walk into the room. I don't want him to point me out to one of the angels and say, "Yes, he's one of mine, even though he doesn't act like it."

So I'm glad I don't have to be uncertain to the answer to the question, *Is God ashamed of me?* The answer is completely under my control. It all depends on whether I consider myself an alien and a stranger in this world and anxiously look forward to heaven. If that is my attitude, then I'll also live like it….

As children of God, we are citizens of heaven. Earth is no longer our home; we long for heaven.

Dave Dravecky

If God takes everything from us, He will never take Himself from us, so long as we do not will it. But more; all our losses and our separations are but for this little moment. Oh truly, for so little a time as this, we ought to have patience.

Francis de Sales

If we died with him, we will also live with him;
If we endure, we will also reign with him.
If we disown him, he will also disown us;
If we are faithless, he will remain faithful,
    for he cannot disown himself....
Do your best to present yourself to God as one approved,
    a workman who does not need to be ashamed
    and who correctly handles the word of truth.

2 Timothy 2:11–13,15

Since we are receiving a kingdom that cannot be shaken,
    let us be thankful,
    and so worship God acceptably with reverence and awe,
    for our "God is a consuming fire."

Hebrews 12:28–29

Many live as enemies of the cross of Christ. Their destiny is destruction, their god is their stomach, and their glory is in their shame. Their mind is on earthly things. But our citizenship is in heaven. And we eagerly await a Savior from there, the Lord Jesus Christ, who, by the power that enables him to bring everything under his control, will transform our lowly bodies so that they will be like his glorious body.

Philippians 3:18–21

Heaven: Our Greatest Homecoming

Do you long for heaven?

Sometimes I get so homesick for heaven that the yearning swells like an ocean wave and I feel as though I'm being swept away, right then and there, to a better country, a heavenly one. Spiritual growth includes an awakening of these deep longings for heaven. This awakening leads to the true contentment of asking less in this life because more is coming in the next. Such longings also heighten our loneliness here on earth.

"Godly people joyfully delight in good things and they nobly endure hard things," says my friend Larry Crabb. "They know that their existence is meaningful and that they are destined for unlimited pleasure at the deepest level. Because they keenly feel that nothing now quite meets the standards of their longing souls, the quiet but throbbing ache within them drives them not to complaint but to anticipation."

Joni Eareckson Tada

Who will be in the throngs of heaven?

I believe there will be more in heaven than in hell. If you ask me why I think so, I answer, because Christ in everything is to have preeminence (Col. 1:18), and I cannot conceive how he could have the preeminence if there are to be more in the dominions of Satan than in paradise. Moreover, it is said there is to be a multitude that no one can number in heaven. I have never read that there is to be a multitude that no one can number in hell. *I rejoice to know that the souls of all infants, as soon as they die, speed their way to paradise. Think what a multitude there is of them!*

Charles H. Spurgeon

And the angel carried me away in the Spirit to a mountain great and high, and showed me the Holy City.... I did not see a temple in the city, because the Lord God Almighty and the Lamb are its temple. The city does not need the sun or the moon to shine on it, for the glory of God gives it light, and the Lamb is its lamp.... Nothing impure will ever enter it, nor will anyone who does what is shameful or deceitful, but only those whose names are written in the Lamb's book of life.

Revelation 21:10,22–23,27

Life: An Eternal Gift, a Lasting Treasure

Clouds of Glory

> Our birth is but a sleep and a forgetting;
> The soul that rises with us, our life's star,
> Hath had elsewhere its setting,
> And cometh from afar;
> Not in entire forgetfulness,
> And not in utter nakedness,
> But trailing clouds of glory do we come
> From God, who is our home.
>
> *William Wordsworth (1770–1850)*

Every friendship, every action, every choice the human soul can make has lasting implications, for we were meant to live forever.

Of all the billions of possibilities, of all the millions of people with whom you could have been best friends, God determined the exact time and place where you should live.

When you consider this amazing fact, your friendships take on a new and profound significance.... Because God has placed you together at this time and in this place, you and your friends have a chance to get a head start on God's eternal plan.

Joni Eareckson Tada

If I can stop one heart from breaking,
I shall not live in vain;
If I can ease one life the aching,
Or cool one pain,
Or help one fainting robin
Unto his nest again,
I shall not live in vain.

Emily Dickinson

For God did not give us a spirit of timidity, but a spirit of power, of love and of self-discipline.... Join with me in suffering for the gospel, by the power of God, who has saved us and called us to a holy life—not because of anything we have done but because of his own purpose and grace. This grace was given us in Christ Jesus before the beginning of time, but it has now been revealed through the appearing of our Savior, Christ Jesus, who has destroyed death and has brought life and immortality to light through the gospel.

2 Timothy 1:7–10

In Patience and Trust You Will Find Strength

Sometimes when we really want something, it is tempting to imagine God is leading us that way. Sometimes God does lead us through our desires. More often, however, as we offer our own desires back to him, he gives us something better. Trust him.

And shall I pray Thee change Thy will, my Father,
Until it be according unto mine?
But no, Lord, no, that never shall be, rather
I pray Thee blend my human will with Thine.

I pray Thee hush the hurrying, eager longing,
I pray Thee soothe the pangs of keen desire—
See in my quiet places, wishes thronging —
Forbid them, Lord, purge, though it be with fire.

And work in me to will and do Thy pleasure
Let all within me, peaceful, reconciled,
Tarry content my Well-Beloved's leisure,
At last, at last, even as a weaned child.

Amy Carmichael

Sometimes even the most willing person, who eagerly desires to serve the Lord, does not know what direction to take. Simply wait—but wait in prayer. He will come at the right time to fulfill His vision for you.

L. B. Cowman

Now faith is being sure of what we hope for and certain of what we do not see. This is what the ancients were commended for. By faith we understand that the universe was formed at God's command, so that what is seen was not made out of what was visible.

By faith Abel offered God a better sacrifice and was commended as a righteous man.

By faith Noah built an ark to save his family and became heir of the righteousness that comes by faith.

By faith Abraham, when called to go, obeyed and went, even though he did not know where he was going.

All these people were still living by faith when they died. They did not receive the things promised; they only saw them and welcomed them from a distance.... God had planned something better for us so that only together with us would they be made perfect.

Therefore, since we are surrounded by such a great cloud of witnesses, let us throw off everything that hinders and the sin that so easily entangles, and let us run with perseverance the race marked out for us. Let us fix our eyes on Jesus, the author and perfecter of our faith, who for the joy set before him endured the cross, scorning its shame, and sat down at the right hand of the throne of God. Consider him who endured such opposition from sinful men, so that you will not grow weary and lose heart.

See Hebrews 11:1–12:3

The Safest Place to Wait Is on Your Knees

Don't know what to do? Just remember: It is truly difficult to fight or run in fear while kneeling. And yet, it is the perfect place to find refuge under "the shadow of His wing."

The movie *Gandhi* contains a fine scene in which Gandhi tries to explain his philosophy to the Presbyterian missionary Charlie Andrews. Walking together in a South African city, the two suddenly find their way blocked by young thugs. Reverend Andrews takes one look at the menacing gangsters and decides to run for it.

Gandhi stops him. "Doesn't the New Testament say if an enemy strikes you on the right cheek you should offer him the left?" Andrews mumbles that he thought the phrase was used metaphorically. "I'm not so sure," Gandhi replies. "I suspect he meant that you must show courage—be willing to take a blow, several blows, to show you will not strike back nor will you be turned aside. And when you do that it calls on something in human nature, something that makes his hatred decrease and his respect increase. I think Christ grasped that and I have seen it work."

Philip Yancey

I do not believe we have even begun to understand the wonderful power there is in being still. We are in such a hurry, always doing, that we are in danger of not allowing God the opportunity to work.

L. B. Cowman

But if you will look to God and plead with the Almighty,
if you are pure and upright,
even now he will rouse himself on your behalf
and restore you to your rightful place.
Your beginnings will seem humble,
so prosperous will your future be.

Job 8:5–7

Let us then approach the throne of grace with confidence, so that we may receive mercy and find grace to help us in our time of need.

Hebrews 4:16

The LORD is my rock, my fortress and my deliverer; my God is my rock, in whom I take refuge. He is my shield and the horn of my salvation, my stronghold.

Psalm 18:2

For you have been my hope, O Sovereign LORD, my confidence since my youth.

Psalm 71:5

PART TWO

Dream Big Dreams

Go confidently in the direction of your dreams!
Live the life you've imagined. As you simplify your
life, the laws of the universe will be simpler.

HENRY DAVID THOREAU

Wait. Just Wait.

The greatest dream is perfected in the loving hand of God. A deliberate, expectant pause is all the invitation God needs to encourage us on ... or check our spirits, preventing us from making the worst of mistakes. So take a deep breath, listen expectantly, and step out with boldness!

I wait.
Dear Lord, Thy ways
Are past finding out,
Thy love too high.
O hold me still
Beneath Thy shadow.
It is enough that Thou
Lift up the light
Of Thy countenance.
I wait—
Because I am commanded
So to do. My mind
Is filled with wonderings.
My soul asks "Why?"
But then the quiet word,
"Wait thou only
Upon God."
And so, not even for the light
To show a step ahead,
But for Thee, dear Lord,
I wait.

Elisabeth Elliot

Early in the morning, as he was on his way back to the city, Jesus was hungry. Seeing a fig tree by the road, he went up to it but found nothing on it except leaves. Then he said to it, "May you never bear fruit again!" Immediately the tree withered.

When the disciples saw this, they were amazed. "How did the fig tree wither so quickly?" they asked.

Jesus replied, "I tell you the truth, if you have faith and do not doubt, not only can you do what was done to the fig tree, but also you can say to this mountain, 'Go, throw yourself into the sea,' and it will be done. If you believe, you will receive whatever you ask for in prayer."

Matthew 21:18–22

I want to know Christ and the power of his resurrection and the fellowship of sharing in his sufferings, becoming like him in his death, and so, somehow, to attain to the resurrection from the dead.

Not that I have already obtained all this, or have already been made perfect, but I press on to take hold of that for which Christ Jesus took hold of me. Brothers, I do not consider myself yet to have taken hold of it. But one thing I do: Forgetting what is behind and straining toward what is ahead, I press on toward the goal to win the prize for which God has called me heavenward in Christ Jesus.

Philippians 3:10–14

God's Plans Are Perfect in Every Way

For a year and a half I diligently studied Korean. I had been invited to teach at a blind school in Seoul, and wanted to be prepared. At the appointed time I applied for my entry visa into Korea, and was confident that in a few short weeks I would be on my way. Two weeks later, the consulate called to say that my application had been denied. No reason was given.

Sure that this was from the evil one, my church family gathered around me and prayed for God to intervene. He didn't. Finally I called the headquarters of my mission sending organization and asked what I should do.

"Well ... would you be willing to go to Africa instead?"

One week later I had swapped my Korean dictionary for a French one, dug out all my summer clothes, and my arm still smarting from all the required shots, arrived in Senegal, West Africa. I later learned that the Senegalese team hadn't wanted any more short-termers. They decided to give me a chance since it was too much trouble to send me back.

Sometimes God shows us his plans by "the scenic route."

Heidi S. Hess

God doesn't want perfect performances but loving persons; he is not a stage manager but a lover. *Being* counts more than *doing,* the singer more than the song. We learn by the mistakes we make and the sufferings they bring. If we haven't made half a dozen mistakes today, we aren't trying hard enough. Even Jesus, according to Scripture, learned obedience "according to suffering." Are we better than he is?

Peter Kreeft

To man belong the plans of the heart,
    but from the LORD comes the reply of the tongue.
All a man's ways seem innocent to him,
    but motives are weighed by the LORD.
Commit to the LORD whatever you do,
    and your plans will succeed.
The LORD works out everything for his own ends—
    even the wicked for a day of disaster.
The LORD detests all the proud of heart.
    Be sure of this: They will not go unpunished.
Through love and faithfulness sin is atoned for;
    through the fear of the LORD a man avoids evil.
When a man's ways are pleasing to the LORD,
    he makes even his enemies live at peace with him.

Proverbs 16:1–7

Prayer: Spiritual "Power Packs" for Our Journey

Righteousness and consistency release the power of prayer.

Don't think you are releasing enough power to accomplish the miraculous by sporadic or casual praying. You are not! You must release the power of God inside of you on a consistent basis…. This verse [in James 5] is telling us, "A prayer of a righteous person is able to do as much as it—the prayer—operates." Our prayers go to work.

Dutch Sheets

Our Lord's lessons and examples teach us that prayer which is not steadfast and persistent, nor revived and refreshed, and does not gather strength from previous prayers, is not the prayer that will triumph.

William Arthur

Prayer and love are learned in the hour when prayer has become impossible and your heart has turned to stone.

Thomas Merton

Our requests, our thoughts, and our prayers are too small; and our expectations are too low. There is no limit to what we may ask and expect of our glorious almighty God.

A. B. Simpson

I will remember the deeds of the LORD;
    yes, I will remember your miracles of long ago.
I will meditate on all your works
    and consider all your mighty deeds.
Your ways, O God, are holy.
    What god is so great as our God?
You are the God who performs miracles;
    you display your power among the peoples.

Psalm 77:11–14

Is any one of you in trouble? He should pray. Is anyone happy?
Let him sing songs of praise. Is any one of you sick? He should
call the elders of the church to pray over him and anoint him with
oil in the name of the Lord. And the prayer offered in faith will
make the sick person well; the Lord will raise him up. If he has
sinned, he will be forgiven. Therefore confess your sins to each
other and pray for each other so that you may be healed. The
prayer of a righteous man is powerful and effective.

James 5:13–16

Pursue True Greatness

There are many kinds of greatness ... but the source of lasting greatness is found in the fountain of holiness.

It has been a privilege to know some of the great men and women of the latter part of this century—people spanning the religious spectrum from Christianity to Buddhism to Judaism to Islam to atheism. Let me stress again, however, that most of my time has been spent with people who will never be in the public eye and yet who are just as important to God as a queen or a president.

True greatness is not measured by the headlines a person commands or the wealth he or she accumulates. The inner character of a person—the undergirding moral and spiritual values and commitments—is the true measure of lasting greatness.

Billy Graham

Our society has gorged itself on the sweet taste of success. We've filled our plates from a buffet of books that range from dressing for success to investing for success. We've passed the newsstands and piled our plates higher with everything from *Gentleman's Quarterly* and *Vogue*, to the *Wall Street Journal* and *Time*.... The irony of all this is that "there is never enough success in anybody's life to make one feel completely satisfied." Instead of fulfillment, we experience the bloated sensation of being full of ourselves—our dreams, our goals, our plans, our projects, our accomplishments. The result of this all-you-can-eat appetite is not contentment. It's nausea. How terribly dissatisfying!

Charles Swindoll

Do not love the world or anything in the world. If anyone loves the world, the love of the Father is not in him. For everything in the world—the cravings of sinful man, the lust of his eyes and the boasting of what he has and does—comes not from the Father but from the world. The world and its desires pass away, but the man who does the will of God lives forever.

1 John 2:15–17

In a large house there are articles not only of gold and silver, but also of wood and clay; some are for noble purposes and some for ignoble. If a man cleanses himself from the latter, he will be an instrument for noble purposes, made holy, useful to the Master and prepared to do any good work. Flee the evil desires of youth, and pursue righteousness, faith, love and peace, along with those who call on the Lord out of a pure heart.

2 Timothy 2:20–22

Those who know your name will trust in you, for you, Lord, have never forsaken those who seek you.

Psalm 9:10

God Gives Us Strength to Live for Him

If being a Christian were a crime, would there be enough evidence to convict you? To live authentic Christian lives, we must go first to the Source of our strength: Jesus.

Sometimes I think we misinterpret faith. In my own life, instead of grabbing hold of what was wrong with it and dealing with it, no matter how painful it was, I acted as if everything were fine…. Jesus never encouraged his friends to cover over the pain in their lives but to bring it into the light, where healing is found.

Sometimes we simply don't want to face the truth about ourselves; the myth reads so much better. Sometimes we do not seek help because it will mean we have to change, and change is painful and unpredictable. To me, now, faith is bringing all that is true about our lives into the blinding light of God's grace. It is believing that he will still be there at the end of the journey. And so will we, perhaps a little bloodied, probably with a limp and possibly, as the Skin Horse [in *The Velveteen Rabbit*] said, with most of our hair loved off, but we will be there.

Sheila Walsh

We are to speak out for what is true and right. Again, to speak out for what is true and right requires more than just railing against evil. The call is for rational, cogent, well-crafted presentations of positive alternatives gleaned from the Scriptures. Is your church encouraging and helping its members to be part of this kind of ministry? Are you honing and then using your own talents and abilities in this kind of ministry? Or is your only response to evil in your community a boycott or gripe session with a few other members of your Bible-study group?

Bob Briner

Therefore, my dear friends … continue to work out your salvation with fear and trembling, for it is God who works in you to will and to act according to his good purpose.

Do everything without complaining or arguing, so that you may become blameless and pure, children of God without fault in a crooked and depraved generation, in which you shine like stars in the universe as you hold out the word of life—in order that I may boast on the day of Christ that I did not run or labor for nothing. But even if I am being poured out like a drink offering on the sacrifice and service coming from your faith, I am glad and rejoice with all of you. So you too should be glad and rejoice with me.

Philippians 2:12–18

For you were once darkness, but now you are light in the Lord. Live as children of light (for the fruit of the light consists in all goodness, righteousness and truth) and find out what pleases the Lord. Have nothing to do with the fruitless deeds of darkness, but rather expose them.

Ephesians 5:8–11

Prayers of Courage, Reflections on Strength

Open, Lord, my inward ear,
And bid my heart rejoice!
Bid my quiet spirit bear
Thy comfortable voice.
Never in the whirlwind found,
Or where earthquakes rock the place;
Still and silent is the sound,
The whisper of Thy grace.
From the world of sin, and noise,
And hurry, I withdraw;
For the small and inward voice
I wait, with humble awe.
Silent am I now, and still,
Dare not in Thy presence move;
To my waiting soul reveal
The secret of Thy love.
Lord, my time is in Thine hand,
My soul to Thee convert;
Thou canst make me understand,
Though I am slow of heart;
Thine, in whom I love and move,
Thine the work, the praise is Thine,
Thou art wisdom, power and love —
And all Thou art is mine.

Charles Wesley

They cried out to the Lord in their trouble,
    and he brought them out of their distress.
He stilled the storm to a whisper;
    the waves of the sea were hushed.
They were glad when it grew calm,
    and he guided them to their desired haven.
Let them give thanks to the Lord for his unfailing love
    and his wonderful deeds for men.
Let them exalt him in the assembly of the people
    and praise him in the council of the elders.

Psalm 107:28–32

Be strong and very courageous. Be careful to obey all the law my servant Moses gave you; do not turn from it to the right or to the left, that you may be successful wherever you go. Do not let this Book of the Law depart from your mouth; meditate on it day and night, so that you may be careful to do everything written in it. Then you will be prosperous and successful. Have I not commanded you? Be strong and courageous. Do not be terrified; do not be discouraged, for the Lord your God will be with you wherever you go.

Joshua 1:7–9

Lord, make me an instrument of thy peace.
Where there is hatred, let me sow love,
Where there is injury, pardon,
Where there is doubt, faith.

Oh Divine Master, grant that I may seek
Not so much to be consoled as to console,
To be understood as to understand,
To be loved as to love another.

For it is in giving that we receive,
It is in pardoning that we are pardoned,
And in dying that we are born to eternal life.

St. Francis of Assisi

At some ideas you stand perplexed, especially at the sight of human sin, uncertain whether to combat it by force or by humble love. Always decide, "I will combat it by humble love." If you make up your mind about that once and for all, you can conquer the whole world.

Fyodor Dostoevsky

It is the branch that bears the fruit
That feels the knife
To prune it for a larger growth,
A fuller life.

Though every budding twig be lopped,
And every grace
Of swaying tendril, springing leaf
Be lost in space,

O thou whose life of joy seems reft,
Of beauty shorn;
Whose aspirations lie in dust,
All bruised and torn,

Rejoice, tho' each desire, each dream,
Each hope of thine
Shall fall and fade; it is the hand
Of love divine

That holds the knife, that cuts and breaks
With tenderest touch,
That thou, whose life has borne some fruit
May'st now bear much.

Annie Johnson Flint

Prayer to the Holy Spirit

Holy Spirit, font of light
Focus of God's glory bright
Shed on us a shining ray.

Father of the fatherless,
Giver of gifts limitless,
Come and touch our hearts today.

Source of strength and sure relief
Comforter in time of grief
Enter in and be our guest.

On our journey grant us aid
Freshening breeze and cooling shade
In our labors inward rest.

Enter each aspiring heart
Occupy its inmost part
With your dazzling purity.

All that gives to us our worth
All that benefits the earth
You bring to maturity.

With your soft, refreshing rains
Break our drought, remove our stains
Bind up all our injuries.

Shake with rushing wind our will
Melt with fire our icy chill
Bring to light our perjuries.

As your promise we believe
Make us ready to receive
Gifts from your unbounded store.

Grant enabling energy
Courage in adversity
Joys that last forevermore.

Author unknown

PART THREE

Ask for Guidance

*The most beautiful thing we can experience
is the mysterious.*

ALBERT EINSTEIN

Hearing God's Voice in Stillness and Solitude

When was the last time you really got away from it all?
No radio, television, or telephone. No immediate goal, apart
from deliberate purposelessness. If you can't
remember the last time you did this, it's time to set
some time apart. It is in these small silences that we
can best hear the voice of God.

Solitude

Laugh, and the world laughs with you,
    Weep, and you weep alone;
For the sad old earth must borrow its mirth,
    But has trouble enough of its own.
Sing, and the hills will answer;
    Sigh, it is lost in the air;
The echoes bound to a joyful sound,
    But shrink from voicing care.

Rejoice, and men will seek you;
    Grieve, and they turn and go;
They want full measure of all your pleasure,
    But they do not need your woe.
Be glad, and your friends are many,
    Be sad, and you lose them all—
There are none to decline your nectared wine,
    But alone you must drink life's gall.

Feast, and your halls are crowded;
    Fast, and the world goes by.
Succeed and give, and it helps you live,
    But no man can help you die.
There is room in the halls of pleasure
    For a large and lordly train,
But one by one we must all file on
    Through the narrow aisles of pain.

Ella Wheeler Wilcox

Turning conviction into action requires great sacrifice, for no one ever comes into the full realization of the best things of God in his spiritual life without learning to walk alone with Him.

L. B. Cowman

The LORD is my shepherd, I shall not be in want.
He makes me lie down in green pastures,
    he leads me beside quiet waters,
    he restores my soul.
He guides me in paths of righteousness for his name's sake.

Psalm 23:1–3

Even in the fastest wheel that is turning, if you look at the center
where the axle is found, there is no movement.
And even in the busiest life
we may dwell alone in eternal stillness.

L. B. Cowman

"I, the LORD, have called you in righteousness;
I will take hold of your hand.
I will keep you and will make you
    to be a covenant for the people
    and a light for the Gentiles,
    to open eyes that are blind,
    to free captives from prison
and to release from the dungeon those who sit in darkness."

Isaiah 42:6–7

Guide me in your truth and teach me,
    for you are God my Savior,
    and my hope is in you all day long.

Psalm 25:5

Since you are my rock and my fortress,
   for the sake of your name lead and guide me.

Psalm 31:3

If I rise on the wings of the dawn, if I settle on the far side of the sea, even there your hand will guide me, your right hand will hold me fast.

Psalm 139:9–10

Got a Decision? Get Counsel!

Graduation marks not only a past achievement, but imminent change ahead. More schooling? Find a job? Which job? When God made Adam, he recognized that "it is not good for man to be alone." So it is with times of transition ... it's never a good idea to make decisions in a vacuum. God wants us to turn to those who can help us figure out the best course of action.

Typically, the young people of a congregation who are called to the professional ministry are singled out for special attention, special counseling, special prayer, and special financial support. Why shouldn't talented young people of the congregation who hope to enter medicine or teaching, or journalism, or writing, or plumbing, or retailing, or any other world of work be given at least the same kind of attention? They should be made to understand that in their careers they have both the possibility and the responsibility to be a part of the ministry of the church. They should be instructed in the how of this as well as the why. Also at the very least they should know that they are valued, being prayed for, and supported as they take the salt of the Gospel to their place of work every day. This is the way to make sure they become roaring lambs.

Bob Briner

Knowledge is a process of piling up facts;
wisdom lies in their simplification.

Martin H. Fischer

He who insists on seeing with perfect clearness before he
decides never decides.

Henri Frederic Amiel

Is not wisdom found among the aged?
Does not long life bring understanding?
To God belong wisdom and power;
counsel and understanding are his.

Job 12:12–13

Wisdom is found on the lips of the discerning,
but a rod is for the back of him who lacks judgment.
Wise men store up knowledge,
but the mouth of a fool invites ruin....
The tongue of the righteous is choice silver,
but the heart of the wicked is of little value.
The lips of the righteous nourish many,
but fools die for lack of judgment.

Proverbs 10:13–14, 20–21

God's Word Is a Sure Light in Life's Darkest Moments

Sometimes rotten things happen. It's a fact of life. And yet, as Christians we have access to a source of comfort and guidance that can get us through our loneliest and hardest times. His Word is an unfailing source of help.

Our capacity to feel, to think, and to experience is so great—to taste the sweetness of joy that life can bring, to bask in the peace of God, to worship on the mountaintops, to ride high on loving and being loved. All of these are wonderful and precious gifts, and I'm so thankful for them as I journey through this earthly life.

But oh, the downfall when we rely on these experiences as the truth or believe them as the absolute. For when the sweetness goes sour, the storm comes raging in, the dryness hits, or the loneliness prevails, we must continually remember that God's truth never changes. My feelings do, my circumstances do, but his truth never does.

Kathy Troccoli

The psalms are a great place to turn when you need a road map through the wilderness. It is somehow encouraging to know that even the great King David, a man after God's own heart, had the same feelings of despair that we do. It somehow lifts our spirits to know that when he was being chased around the literal desert at the point of King Saul's spear, he struggled with his relationship to God. This man whom Scripture calls "the apple of God's eye" sometimes felt like a bowl of rotten fruit.

Although I resonate with David's questions and fears and pleas in the first two-thirds of Psalm 13, I rest in his final two verses: "But I trust in your unfailing love; my heart rejoices in your salvation. I will sing to the Lord, for he has been good to me."

Dave Dravecky

Your word is a lamp to my feet
and a light for my path.
I have taken an oath and confirmed it,
that I will follow your righteous laws.
I have suffered much;
preserve my life, O Lᴏʀᴅ, according to your word.
Accept, O Lᴏʀᴅ, the willing praise of my mouth,
and teach me your laws.
Though I constantly take my life in my hands,
I will not forget your law....
My heart is set on keeping your decrees
to the very end.

Psalm 119:105–9, 112

Following God ... Even When We Can't See Clearly

The most spiritual men and women have difficulty discerning God's guiding hand from time to time. In those silences we learn to trust him more. In the two passages below, two famous Christians share the advice their mothers gave them on remaining sensitive to God's leading.

He who hath led will lead
All through the wilderness,
He who hath fed will surely feed....
He who hath heard thy cry
Will never close His ear,
He who hath marked thy faintest sigh
Will not forget thy tear.
He loveth always, faileth never,
So rest on Him today—forever.

Amy Carmichael

I know that I know Jesus Christ," I wrote to Mother, "but I've lost my feeling. I can't seem to get anywhere in prayer. I don't feel anything."

"Son, God is testing you," she wrote back. "He tells us to walk not by feeling but by faith, and when you don't feel anything, God may be closer to you than before. Through the darkness and through the fog, put your hand up by faith. You'll sense the touch of God."

Billy Graham

When they had finished eating, Jesus said to Simon Peter, "Simon son of John, do you truly love me more than these?"

"Yes, Lord," he said, "you know that I love you."

Jesus said, "Feed my lambs."

Again Jesus said, "Simon son of John, do you truly love me?"

He answered, "Yes, Lord, you know that I love you."

Jesus said, "Take care of my sheep."

The third time he said to him, "Simon son of John, do you love me?"

Peter was hurt because Jesus asked him the third time, "Do you love me?" He said, "Lord, you know all things, you know that I love you."

Jesus said, "Feed my sheep. I tell you the truth, when you were younger you dressed yourself and went where you wanted; but when you are old you will stretch out your hands, and someone else will dress you and lead you where you do not want to go." Jesus said this to indicate the kind of death by which Peter would glorify God. Then he said to him, "Follow me!"

John 21:15–19

Chocolate or French Vanilla?

Some well-intentioned Christians take "finding God's will" to an extreme. Finding the balance between seeking God's guidance and using common sense is an important part of reaching Christian maturity.

Shortly after finishing Bible school, I was given a choice between going overseas for a year, and continuing to work at my current job. Both options had pros and cons, and I was determined to dig my heels in until I heard directly from God on the matter. I prayed and prayed, "So, God, what do YOU want me to do?"

My answer came unexpectedly. I was working late one night when the janitor came in to my office and struck up a conversation. When I told him of my dilemma, he leaned against his broom and studied me thoughtfully. "Have you ever considered that maybe God doesn't have a strong opinion, one way or the other?"

I hadn't considered this. "Is that possible?"

"Well," he said, "when I take my children out to the ice cream parlor, I tell them that they can pick any kind of ice cream they want. One scoop, any flavor. Now, what if my kid said to me, 'Dad, you pick. You know what's best.'"

I had no idea. "What would you say?"

"I'd tell her, 'Part of growing up is learning to make decisions for yourself, and dealing with the consequences. You pick.'"

Sometimes the only way to tell if there's an open door is to try to step through it.

Heidi S. Hess

I lift my eyes to the hills—where does my help come from?
My help comes from the Lord, the Maker of heaven and earth.

Psalm 121:1–2

Ask and it will be given to you; seek and you will find; knock and
the door will be opened to you. For everyone who asks receives;
he who seeks finds; and to him who knocks, the door will be
opened.

Which of you, if his son asks for bread, will give him a stone?
Or if he asks for a fish, will give him a snake? If you, then, though
you are evil, know how to give good gifts to your children, how
much more will your Father in heaven give good gifts to those
who ask him! So in everything, do to others what you would have
them do to you, for this sums up the Law and the Prophets.

Matthew 7:7–12

In your unfailing love you will lead
    the people you have redeemed.

Exodus 15:13

The Secret to Finding God's Will

Quite often I meet Christians who tend to wear their spirituality as an aura of otherworldliness. According to some, the most spiritual Christian is one who confidently asserts, "God told me it's time to buy a new dress," or "I'm positive God wants our church to use our money this way." "God told me" can become a casual manner of speech. Actually, I believe that most of what God has to say to me is already written in the Bible, and the onus is on me to study diligently His will revealed there. For most of us, mysterious direct messages from a hotline to God are not the ordinary ways of discerning His will. Guidance mediated through circumstances or modified on the advice of wise Christian friends, though it may seem less spectacular, is not at all inferior.

College graduates agonize over what decisions to make for the future, waiting for God to alert them with a jolting, custom-made plan dropped into their laps. In the Bible God indeed employed the supernatural means of angels and visions and the like to convey His will. But if you look closely at those incidents, you will note that few of them came in response to prayer for guidance. They were usually unrequested and unexpected.... The individual Christian would better spend his time working on practical, daily obedience to what God has already revealed rather than fervent searches for some magic secret, elusive as the Holy Grail.

Dr. Paul Brand

Be still, my soul—thy God doth undertake
To guide the future as He has the past;
Thy hope, thy confidence let nothing shake —
All now mysterious shall be bright at last.
Be still, my soul—the waves and winds still know
His voice who ruled them while he dwelt below.

Katharina von Schlegel

The power of the Christian life hinges on one thing.
That one thing is taking God at His word,
believing He really means what He says;
and accepting the very words that reveal His goodness and grace.

Adam Clarke

I desire to do your will, O my God; your law is within my heart.

Psalm 40:8

Reach Out and Touch ...

God's greatness exceeds human comprehension. For this reason he meets us not mind to mind, but heart to heart.

Our intense need to understand will always be a powerful stumbling block to our attempts to reach God in simple love, and must always be overcome.

For if you do not overcome this need to understand it will undermine your quest.

It will replace the darkness which you have pierced to reach God with clear images of something which, however good, however beautiful, however Godlike, is not God....

Do not misunderstand. Simple, sudden thoughts of good and spiritual things are not wrong.

But in our effort to pierce the dark cloud of unknowing, to reach out spontaneously to God, they can be a hindrance.

For surely in our efforts to have God perfectly, we must not be content to rest in the mere consciousness of any thing that is not God.

> Anonymous
> *Where Only Love Can Go*

God loves questions. He says He rewards those who earnestly seek Him. He never casts His pearls before pigs; He hides them in parables, in riddles, in questions, so that those who really want to know will ask. He wants us to come right after it; He wants us to ask why. But no one is asking the right questions anymore.

Rarely do I encounter a student today who is after knowledge and truth for its own sake. College is no longer sought for the widening of one's perspective but for the narrowing of one's abilities toward a specialized job that will translate directly in the marketplace.... To grow, to widen, to investigate, to challenge, to climb an intellectual mountain just because it's there are foreign concepts to this student generation. Methods are more important than meaning. "How?" is more important than "Why?"

John Fischer

"But where can wisdom be found?
Where does understanding dwell?
Man does not comprehend its worth;
it cannot be found in the land of the living.
The deep says, 'It is not in me';
the sea says, 'It is not with me.'
It cannot be bought with the finest gold,
nor can its price be weighed in silver....
God understands the way to it
and he alone knows where it dwells,
for he views the ends of the earth
and sees everything under the heavens.

When he established the force of the wind
and measured out the waters,
when he made a decree for the rain
and a path for the thunderstorm,
then he looked at wisdom and appraised it;
he confirmed it and tested it.
And he said to man,
'The fear of the Lord—that is wisdom,
and to shun evil is understanding.'"

Job 28:12–15, 23–28

Then I saw a new heaven and a new earth, for the first heaven and the first earth had passed away, and there was no longer any sea. I saw the Holy City, the new Jerusalem, coming down out of heaven from God, prepared as a bride beautifully dressed for her husband. And I heard a loud voice from the throne saying, "Now the dwelling of God is with men, and he will live with them. They will be his people, and God himself will be with them and be their God. He will wipe every tear from their eyes. There will be no more death or mourning or crying or pain, for the old order of things has passed away."

Revelation 21:1–4

Do not be anxious about anything, but in everything, by prayer and petition, with thanksgiving, present your requests to God. And the peace of God, which transcends all understanding, will guard your hearts and your minds in Christ Jesus.

Philippians 4:6–7

The fear of the LORD is the beginning of wisdom;
    all who follow his precepts have good understanding.

Psalm 111:10

PART FOUR

Accept God's Good Gifts

The only gift is a portion of thyself.

Ralph Waldo Emerson

Receive God's Good Gifts

It just didn't feel like Christmas. The warm African sun on my face was pleasant enough, but the prospects of snow were slim indeed. And in the predominantly Muslim country of Senegal, the sights and sounds of Christmas were strangely absent. Unless you counted the tired looking Father Christmas that hung, pinata-like, from the European grocery store downtown.

Desperate for something to lift my spirits, I went into the *Supermarche* and bought a bag of oranges, then started passing them out to children on the street. The next thing I knew, I was engulfed by a mass of clutching, grabbing humanity. Full-grown adults pushed youngsters out of the way to snatch one of the mottled orange-and-brown orbs from my hands. Then another, and another, until the fruit was gone. Merry Christmas. *What would it take*, I wondered, *to get a reaction like this at home? Those oranges would have to be dipped in platinum!*

Yes, we can be a thankless bunch. The more God gives us, the more we demand. "Thanks for the parking spot, God. Now if you could just help me negotiate that raise with my boss...." Still, He keeps giving. These next few pages contain just a smattering of the many, many reasons we have to be truly thankful.

Heidi S. Hess

Blessed are you who are poor,
for yours is the kingdom of God.
Blessed are you who hunger now,
for you will be satisfied.
Blessed are you who weep now,
for you will laugh.
Blessed are you when men hate you,
when they exclude you and insult you
and reject your name as evil, because of the Son of Man.
Rejoice in that day and leap for joy, because great is your reward
in heaven.
For that is how their fathers treated the prophets.

Luke 6:20–23

Don't be deceived, my dear brothers. Every good and perfect gift is from above, coming down from the Father of the heavenly lights, who does not change like shifting shadows. He chose to give us birth through the word of truth, that we might be a kind of first-fruits of all he created.

James 1:16–18

The Gifts of Mercy and Forgiveness

In A Severe Mercy, *Sheldon Vanauken paints an unforgettable portrait of human love at its most sublime. He later wrote* Under the Mercy, *in which he shares another love story: the story of his journey into the heart of God. In this passage Vanauken reveals one of the most compelling attributes of our holy God.*

We are told to hate the sin and love the sinner. That, I think, is one of the very hardest things for Christians to do: to keep the two parts in balance. One set of Christians hate the sin and, in effect, hate the sinner as well by refusing to understand and love him. The other set of Christians love the sinner—the homosexual, for instance, or the woman who has an abortion—so enthusiastically that they love the sin also by denying it to be sin. Both sets deny the Lord....

The examination of my life represented by this book ... has convinced me that I have lived—and shall live and die—under the Mercy. The Mercy, which is to say the Love, is *there*. Undeserved. We are *all* under the Mercy, the deserving and the undeserving alike.... The Mercy—that word means so much to me, having such need of it—is simply the charity of God. The forgiving love when we know not what we do; and the more gladly forgiving love when we do know and are penitent.

Sheldon Vanauken

Love your enemies, do good to them, and lend to them without expecting to get anything back. Then your reward will be great, and you will be sons of the Most High, because he is kind to the ungrateful and wicked. Be merciful, just as your Father is merciful. Do not judge, and you will not be judged. Do not condemn, and you will not be condemned. Forgive, and you will be forgiven. Give, and it will be given to you. A good measure, pressed down, shaken together and running over, will be poured into your lap. For with the measure you use, it will be measured to you.

Luke 6:35–38

Will the Lord be pleased with thousands of rams,
    with ten thousand rivers of oil?
Shall I offer my firstborn for my transgression,
    the fruit of my body for the sin of my soul?
He has showed you, O man, what is good.
    And what does the Lord require of you?
To act justly and to love mercy
    and to walk humbly with your God.

Micah 6:7–8

If you forgive men when they sin against you,
    your heavenly Father will also forgive you.
But if you do not forgive men their sins,
    your Father will not forgive your sins.

Matthew 6:14–15

God's gift of mercy is a favorite theme of many of the great-est Christian hymn writers. Their lyrics reflect the wonder of being touched by such a great gift of grace.

There's a wideness in God's mercy like the wideness of the sea;
There's a kindness in his justice that is more than liberty.
There is welcome for the sinner, and more graces for the good;
There is mercy with the Savior, there is healing in his blood.

Frederick W. Faber

Depth of mercy can there be mercy still reserved for me?
Can my God his wrath forbear—me, the chief of sinners, spare?
There for me my Savior stands, holding forth his wounded hands;
God is love! I know, I feel. Jesus weeps and loves me still.

Charles Wesley

Come, Thou Fount of every blessing, tune my heart to sing Thy
    grace;
Streams of mercy never ceasing, call for songs of loudest praise.
Teach me some melodious sonnet sung by flaming tongues above;
Praise the mount—I'm fixed upon it—mount of Thy redeeming
    love.

Robert Robinson

A few days later, when Jesus again entered Capernaum, the people heard that he had come home. So many gathered that there was no room left, not even outside the door, and he preached the word to them. Some men came, bringing to him a paralytic, carried by four of them. Since they could not get him to Jesus because of the crowd, they made an opening in the roof above Jesus and, after digging through it, lowered the mat the paralyzed man was lying on. When Jesus saw their faith, he said to the paralytic, "Son, your sins are forgiven."

Now some teachers of the law were sitting there, thinking to themselves, "Why does this fellow talk like that? He's blaspheming! Who can forgive sins but God alone?"

Immediately Jesus knew in his spirit that this was what they were thinking in their hearts, and he said to them, "Why are you thinking these things? Which is easier: to say to the paralytic, 'Your sins are forgiven,' or to say, 'Get up, take your mat and walk'? But that you may know that the Son of Man has authority on earth to forgive sins. ..." He said to the paralytic, "I tell you, get up, take your mat and go home." He got up, took his mat and walked out in full view of them all. This amazed everyone and they praised God, saying, "We have never seen anything like this!"

Mark 2:1–12

The Gift of Salvation

Salvation is not a blessing to be enjoyed on the death bed, or to be sung about in a future state. Salvation is to be obtained, received, promised, and enjoyed now....

This complete salvation is accompanied by a holy calling. Those the Savior called on the cross are in due time effectively called to holiness by the power of God the Holy Spirit. Thus they leave their sins and endeavor to be like Christ. They choose holiness, not out of compulsion, but from the impulse of a new nature that leads them to rejoice in holiness as naturally as they formerly delighted in sin.

God did not call us because we are holy. He called us that we might be holy. Holiness is the beauty produced by His workmanship. The excellencies we see in a believer are as much the work of God as the atonement itself. Thus the fullness of the grace of God is brought out.

Salvation must be of grace, because the Lord is the author of it.... This is the believer's privilege—a present salvation. This is the believer's calling—a holy life.

Charles H. Spurgeon

Redeemed—how I love to proclaim it!
Redeemed by the blood of the Lamb;
Redeemed thru His infinite mercy —
His child, and forever, I am.
Redeemed, redeemed, redeemed by the blood of the Lamb.
Redeemed, redeemed, His child, and forever, I am!

Fanny Crosby

And I looked and there before me was a great multitude that no one could count, from every nation, tribe, people and language, standing before the throne and in front of the Lamb. They were wearing white robes and were holding palm branches in their hands. And they cried out in a loud voice:

"Salvation belongs to our God,
who sits on the throne,
and to the Lamb."

Revelation 7:9–10

But we see Jesus, who was made a little lower than the angels, now crowned with glory and honor because he suffered death, so that by the grace of God he might taste death for everyone. In bringing many sons to glory, it was fitting that God, for whom and through whom everything exists, should make the author of their salvation perfect through suffering. Both the one who makes men holy and those who are made holy are of the same family. So Jesus is not ashamed to call them brothers.

Hebrews 2:9–11

71

The Gift of Joy

*The gift of "joy" must never be confused with a temporal
state of mere happiness. For the Christian, joy is a state of
mind that transcends our immediate circumstances. Paul
experienced it in prison. Others experience it in the midst of
grave financial hardship or physical suffering. Joy is the
result of placing the things that make us most anxious into
the loving hands of our heavenly Father ... and leaving
them there.*

No heaven can come to us unless our hearts rest in it today.
Take heaven. No peace lies in the future that is not hidden in
this precious little instant. Take peace. The gloom of the world is
but a shadow. Behind it, within our reach, is joy. . . . Life is so
generous a giver, but we, judging its gifts by their coverings, cast
them away as ugly or heavy or hard. Remove the covering and
you will find beneath it a living splendor, woven of love and
wisdom and power. Welcome it, greet it, and touch the angel's
hand that brings it.

Everything we call a trial, a sorrow, a duty: believe me, that
angel's hand is there, the gift is there, and the wonder of an over-
shadowing Presence. Our joys too: be not content with them as
joys. They too conceal diviner gifts. Life is so full of meaning and
purpose, so full of beauty beneath its covering, that you will find

earth but cloaks your heaven. Courage, then, to claim it, that's all! But courage you have, and the knowledge that we are pilgrims wending through unknown country on our way home.

Joni Eareckson Tada

L aughter is the sun that drives winter from the human face.

Victor Hugo

Clap your hands, all you nations;
    shout to God with cries of joy.
How awesome is the LORD Most High,
    the great King over all the earth!
God has ascended amid shouts of joy,
    the LORD amid the sounding of trumpets.
Sing praises to God, sing praises;
    sing praises to our King, sing praises.
For God is King of all the earth;
    sing to him a psalm of praise.
God reigns over the nations;
    God is seated on his holy throne.

Psalm 47:1–2, 5–8

Make sure that nobody pays back wrong for wrong, but always try to be kind to each other and to everyone else. Be joyful always; pray continually; give thanks in all circumstances, for this is God's will for you in Christ Jesus.

1 Thessalonians 5:15–18

Dear friends, do not be surprised at the painful trial you are suffering, as though something strange were happening to you. But rejoice that you participate in the sufferings of Christ, so that you may be overjoyed when his glory is revealed. If you are insulted because of the name of Christ, you are blessed, for the Spirit of glory and of God rests on you....Those who suffer according to God's will should commit themselves to their faithful Creator and continue to do good.

1 Peter 4:12–14, 19

A woman giving birth to a child has pain because her time has come; but when her baby is born she forgets the anguish because of her joy that a child is born into the world. So with you: Now is your time of grief, but I will see you again and you will rejoice, and no one will take away your joy.

John 16:21–22

You will go out in joy
    and be led forth in peace;
the mountains and hills
    will burst into song before you,
and all the trees of the field
    will clap their hands.

Isaiah 55:12

Shout for joy, O heavens;
    rejoice, O earth;
    burst into song, O mountains!
For the LORD comforts his people
    and will have compassion on his afflicted ones.

Isaiah 49:13

The Gift of Humility

Humility is one of the most distinctive qualities of the mature Christian life. Paul tells us that Jesus did not consider equality with God something to be grasped, but "humbled himself ...." How can we, as children of the King, do any less?

We must not think Pride is something God forbids because He is offended at it, or that Humility is something He demands as due to His own dignity—as if God Himself was proud. He is not in the least worried about His own dignity. The point is, He wants you to know Him: wants to give you Himself. And He and you are two things of such a kind that if you really get into any kind of touch with Him you will, in fact, be humble—delightedly humble.

C. S. Lewis

I long to accomplish a great and noble task, but it is my chief duty to accomplish humble tasks as though they were great and noble. The world is moved along, not only by the mighty shoves of its heroes, but also by the aggregate of the tiny pushes of each honest worker.

Helen Keller

Humility is perfect quietness of heart. It is to expect nothing, to wonder at nothing that is done to me, to feel nothing done against me. It is to be at rest when nobody praises me, and when I am blamed or despised.

Andrew Murray

Brothers, if someone is caught in a sin, you who are spiritual should restore him gently. But watch yourself, or you also may be tempted. Carry each other's burdens, and in this way you will fulfill the law of Christ. If anyone thinks he is something when he is nothing, he deceives himself. Each one should test his own actions. Then he can take pride in himself, without comparing himself to somebody else, for each one should carry his own load.

Galatians 6:1–5

Your attitude should be the same as that of Christ Jesus:
Who, being in very nature God,
did not consider equality with God something to be grasped,
but made himself nothing,
taking the very nature of a servant,
being made in human likeness.
And being found in appearance as a man,
he humbled himself
and became obedient to death—
even death on a cross!

Philippians 2:5–8

The Gift of Peace

The peace of God is an eternal calm like the cushion of the sea. It lies so deeply within the human heart that no external difficulty or disturbance can reach it. And anyone who enters the presence of God becomes a partaker of that undisturbed and undisturbable calm.

Arthur Tappan Pierson

Like a river glorious is God's perfect peace,
Over all victorious in its bright increase;
Perfect, yet it floweth fuller every day,
Perfect yet it groweth deeper all the way.

Every joy or trial falleth from above,
Traced upon our dial by the Sun of Love;
We may trust him fully all for us to do —
They who trust him wholly find him wholly true.

Stayed upon Jehovah, hearts are fully blest—
Finding, as he promised perfect peace and rest.

Frances R. Havergal

If there is righteousness in the heart, there will be beauty in the character. If there be beauty in the character, there will be harmony in the home. If there is harmony in the home, there will be order in the nation. If there is order in the nation, there will be peace in the world.

Old Chinese Proverb

Peace I leave with you; my peace I give you. I do not give to you as the world gives. Do not let your hearts be troubled and do not be afraid.

John 14:27

Make every effort to live in peace with all men and to be holy; without holiness no one will see the Lord.

Hebrews 12:14

Therefore, since we have been justified through faith, we have peace with God through our Lord Jesus Christ, through whom we have gained access by faith into this grace in which we now stand. And we rejoice in the hope of the glory of God. Not only so, but we also rejoice in his sufferings, because we know that suffering produces perseverance; perseverance, character; and character, hope. And hope does not disappoint us, because God has poured out his love into our hearts by the Holy Spirit, whom he has given us.

Romans 5:1–5

The Gifts of Faith and Provision

> *There is an unmistakable connection between believing that God will take care of you ... and receiving his provision. Not that he always supplies in the way or time frame we had in mind. But his timing is always perfect, and his gifts are always best.*

Faith is acting on the invisible, but not an abstract invisible! It is seeing Him, the Creator Who is a person.... It is not some vague optimism.... There is to be a life of faith, a life of faith not only at certain climactic moments, but a life of faith in not forgetting what faith is.... It is believing the promises of the Creator of the world, and acting upon them.

Francis Schaeffer

When we pray, "Hallowed be Your name," we are really claiming a miracle in the ordinary. We are asking that all of life be filled with God's name, that is, with His presence and power....

As we pray this petition, we mean that we claim every moment, relationship, and situation in life as His gift. They are holy because they belong to Him. That immediately changes our thinking. Instead of living in the past or looking to the future, "now" becomes the most important moment of our lives. We can experience what the eighteenth-century Jesuit Jean-Pierre de

Caussarde called "the sacrament of the present moment." The Lord wants to bless every second with His holy presence and guidance in whatever happens to us.

Lloyd Ogilvie

Whether or not we sense and feel the presence of the Holy Spirit
  or one of the holy angels,
  by faith we are certain
God will never leave us or forsake us.

Billy Graham

Jesus said, "I tell you that if two of you on earth agree about anything you ask for, it will be done for you by my Father in heaven. For where two or three come together in my name, there am I with them."

Matthew 18:19–20

I am the LORD, the God of all mankind. Is anything too hard for me?

Jeremiah 32:27

The Gift of Abundance

The cancer had taken not only my sister's leg, but most of my family's finances as well. I lay awake that Saturday night, listening to my parents talk in hushed tones in their room, and wondered what we were going to do. On Monday morning our visitors would arrive, the parents of our Finnish exchange student, Jaana. And we didn't know how we were going to feed them. An unexpected medical bill had arrived that week, and drained the last few dollars from the checking account. It was going to be a long week. Fitfully, I drifted off to sleep.

The next morning Dad gathered us around and gave us strict instructions that we were not to mention our predicament to anyone at the church. They had done enough already. Then he bowed his head and asked God to help us.

Three hours later when we arrived home from church, I noticed that the front porch door was propped open. Cautiously we climbed the stairs ... and gasped, in unison. There on the porch were nine large boxes of groceries, crowned with a delectable three-layered chocolate cake! Enough food to last us at least a month!

We never found out who delivered the food. But we all knew Who had provided for us. We had trusted God to take care of us. And he responded from the abundance of His heart.

Heidi S. Hess

Praise our God, O peoples,
    let the sound of his praise be heard;
he has preserved our lives
    and kept our feet from slipping.
For you, O God, tested us;
    you refined us like silver.
You brought us into prison
    and laid burdens on our backs.
You let men ride over our heads;
    we went through fire and water,
    but you brought us to a place of abundance.

Psalm 66:8–12

Great is the LORD and most worthy of praise;
    his greatness no one can fathom.
One generation will commend your works to another;
    they will tell of your mighty acts.
They will speak of the glorious splendor of your majesty,
    and I will meditate on your wonderful works.
They will tell of the power of your awesome works,
    and I will proclaim your great deeds.
They will celebrate your abundant goodness
    and joyfully sing of your righteousness.

Psalm 145:3–7

For if, by the trespass of the one man, death reigned through that one man, how much more will those who receive God's abundant provision of grace and of the gift of righteousness reign in life through the one man, Jesus Christ.

Romans 5:17

Do not throw away your confidence; it will be richly rewarded. You need to persevere so that when you have done the will of God, you will receive what he has promised. For in just a very little while,
"He who is coming will come and will not delay.
But my righteous one will live by faith.
And if he shrinks back,
I will not be pleased with him."

Hebrews 10:35–38

Great peace have they who love your law,
and nothing can make them stumble.

Psalm 119:165

I will praise the LORD, who counsels me;
even at night my heart instructs me.

Psalm 16:7

You will keep in perfect peace
him whose mind is steadfast,
because he trusts in you.

Isaiah 26:3

The fruit of righteousness will be peace;
    the effect of righteousness will bequietness and
        confidence forever.

Isaiah 32:17

Peace I leave with you; my peace I give you. I do not give to you
as the world gives. Do not let your hearts be troubled and do not
be afraid.

John 14:27

The Gift of Contentment

The secret of contentment lies in discovering who in the world you are—and mobilizing your courage to be that person.

The richest and deepest contentment is a natural result of achieving authenticity—that is, knowing yourself intimately, appreciating your unique gifts and abilities, and making choices moment by moment that demonstrate honor and respect for yourself....

Instinctively, you know that small doses of happiness are a far stretch from contentment. Contentment has its roots way down at the center of yourself, where your consciousness is headquartered, where you perceive, think, feel, and dream. Happiness doesn't go nearly as deep. *Contentment* is almost always the consequence of your relationship with yourself, a consistent loyalty to the person you truly are.

Neil Clark Warren

True contentment is a thing as active as agriculture. It is the power of getting out of any situation all that there is in it. It is arduous and it is rare.

G. K. Chesterton

Never be afraid to trust an unknown future to an all-knowing God.

Corrie ten Boom

A cheerful heart is good medicine, but a crushed spirit dries up the bones.

Proverbs 17:22

Godliness with contentment is great gain. For we brought nothing into the world, and we can take nothing out of it. But if we have food and clothing, we will be content with that. People who want to get rich fall into temptation and a trap and into many foolish and harmful desires that plunge men into ruin and destruction. For the love of money is a root of all kinds of evil. Some people, eager for money, have wandered from the faith and pierced themselves with many griefs.

1 Timothy 6:6–10

I rejoice greatly in the Lord that at last you have renewed your concern for me. Indeed, you have been concerned, but you had no opportunity to show it. I am not saying this because I am in need, for I have learned to be content whatever the circumstances. I know what it is to be in need, and I know what it is to have plenty. I have learned the secret of being content in any and every situation, whether well fed or hungry, whether living in plenty or in want. I can do everything through him who gives me strength.

Philippians 4:10–13

The Gift of Freedom

*From the moment we are drawn into the Kingdom, the rest
of our lives are spent embracing the freedom Christ has won
for us, and leading others to release their shackles as well.
The cords that bind our hearts to His are not the steel
shackles of bondage, but the silken strands of love.*

We must leisurely say goodbye to the world, and little by little
draw our affections from creatures. Trees that the wind
tears up are not suitable to transplant, because they leave their
roots in the earth; but he who would carry trees into another soil
must skillfully disengage little by little all the roots one after the
other. And since from this miserable land we are to be trans-
planted from that of the living, we must withdraw and disengage
our affections one after the other from this world. I do not say
that we must roughly break all the ties we have formed ... but we
must unsew and untie them.

Francis de Sales

Keeping Christ bottled up in the churches is keeping salt in the
shakers, and He does not go where we do not take Him. We
need to take Him everywhere and show His relevance and the
relevance of His Word to every aspect of modern life. This is not
an option, it is ... a scriptural imperative.

Bob Briner

It is for freedom that Christ has set us free. Stand firm, then, and do not let yourselves be burdened again by a yoke of slavery.

Galatians 5:1

Since we have such a hope, we are very bold. We are not like Moses, who would put a veil over his face to keep the Israelites from gazing at it while the radiance was fading away. But their minds were made dull, for to this day the same veil remains when the old covenant is read. It has not been removed, because only in Christ is it taken away. Even to this day when Moses is read, a veil covers their hearts. But whenever anyone turns to the Lord, the veil is taken away. Now the Lord is the Spirit, and where the Spirit of the Lord is, there is freedom.

2 Corinthians 3:12–17

Live as free men, but do not use your freedom as a cover-up for evil; live as servants of God. Show proper respect to everyone: Love the brotherhood of believers, fear God, honor the king.

1 Peter 2:16–17

The Gift of Love

The supreme irony is that although God is altogether lovely, as fallen creatures we do not love Him. He is worthy and deserves our love. We owe Him our love, yet we do not love Him. On the other side, we are altogether unlovely by His standards. There is nothing in us to commend us to God, and He certainly does not owe us His love. But the staggering fact remains, *He loves us*. He loves us to the extent that He gave His only begotten Son for us.

R. C. Sproul

No virtue is really virtue unless it is permeated by love.
Justice without love is legalism.
Faith without love is ideology.
Hope without love is self-centeredness.
Forgiveness without love is self-abasement.
Fortitude without love is recklessness.
Generosity without love is extravagance.
Care without love is obligation.
Fidelity without love is servitude.

Richard McBrient

Happiness is about having someone to love you, in a way—if the someone is really Someone. Augustine's famous metaphor is that we all have a vacuum inside us that only God can fill. Occasionally now you hear an expression used in addiction and recovery circles that each of us has a "hole in our souls." C. S. Lewis said that we bear, all our lives, an "inconsolable longing," an innate awareness of our incompleteness that is, ultimately, only resolved when we are present with the Lord.

Stacy & Paula Rinehart

Praise be to the LORD,
 for he showed his wonderful love to me
 when I was in a besieged city.
In my alarm I said,
 "I am cut off from your sight!"
Yet you heard my cry for mercy
 when I called to you for help.
Love the LORD, all his saints!
 The LORD preserves the faithful,
 but the proud he pays back in full.
Be strong and take heart,
 all you who hope in the LORD.

Psalm 31:21–24

As the Father has loved me, so have I loved you. Now remain in my love. If you obey my commands, you will remain in my love, just as I have obeyed my Father's commands and remain in his love. I have told you this so that my joy may be in you and that your joy may be complete. My command is this: Love each other as I have loved you. Greater love has no one than this, that he lay down his life for his friends. You are my friends if you do what I command. I no longer call you servants, because a servant does not know his master's business. Instead, I have called you friends, for everything that I learned from my Father I have made known to you. You did not choose me, but I chose you and appointed you to go and bear fruit—fruit that will last. Then the Father will give you whatever you ask in my name. This is my command: Love each other.

John 15:9–17

May the God of hope fill you with all joy and peace as you trust in him, so that you may overflow with hope by the power of the Holy Spirit.

Romans 15:13

But the fruit of the Spirit is love, joy, peace, patience, kindness, goodness, faithfulness.

Galatians 5:22

The Gift of Suffering

When we are in the throes of some physical or emotional trauma, it can be difficult to appreciate the "gift" of suffering. And yet, it is in the darkest times of our life when the light of God's love seems to shine the brightest, for it is at those times we depend upon it the most.

Where is God when it hurts?

He has been there from the beginning, designing a pain system that, even in the midst of a fallen world, still bears the stamp of his genius and equips us for life on this planet.

He transforms pain, using it to teach and strengthen us, if we allow it to turn us toward him....

He has joined us. He has hurt and bled and cried and suffered. He has dignified for all time those who suffer, by sharing their pain.

He is with us now, ministering to us through his Spirit and through members of his body who are commissioned to bear us up and relieve our suffering for the sake of the head.

He is waiting, gathering the armies of good. One day he will unleash them, and the world will see one last terrifying moment of suffering before the full victory is ushered in. Then, God will create for us a new, incredible world. And pain shall be no more.

Philip Yancey

Those who don't know how to weep with their whole heart, don't know how to laugh either.

Golda Meir

The cross is never found in a beautiful room, but in Calvary. Those who want to belong to Jesus have to feel happy to walk with him. No matter how painful it is, we have to share his passion.

Mother Teresa

God is our refuge and strength, an ever-present help in trouble.

Psalm 46:1

Endure hardship as discipline; God is treating you as sons.... Our fathers disciplined us for a little while as they thought best; but God disciplines us for our good, that we may share in his holiness. No discipline seems pleasant at the time, but painful. Later on, however, it produces a harvest of righteousness and peace for those who have been trained by it.

Hebrews 12:7, 10–11

It is true that "whole, unbruised, unbroken men are of little use to God." In the here and now He cannot greatly use those who are hard, unloving, and self-centered. But God is not interested in brokenness primarily for its temporal value, great as that may be. His Bride-elect is in training for the throne. She is in the school of suffering to learn agape love to qualify her for rulership in an economy where the law of love is supreme. This is why God is willing to take a lifetime to teach her love.

Paul Billheimer

People desire only the strong, successful, victorious, and unbroken things in life. But heaven is being filled with earth's broken lives, and there is no "bruised reed" that Christ cannot take and restore.

J. R. Miller

Strength comes from struggle; weakness from ease.

B. C. Forbes

There is no remedy in this tempest but to wait for the mercy of God. For at an unexpected time, with one word alone or a chance happening, He so quickly calms the storm that it seems there had not been even as much as a cloud in that soul, and it remains filled with sunlight and much more consolation. And like one who has escaped from a dangerous battle and been victorious, it comes out praising our Lord; for it was He who fought for the victory.

Teresa of Avila

Surely he took up our infirmities and carried our sorrows,
    yet we considered him stricken by God,
    smitten by him, and afflicted.
But he was pierced for our transgressions,
    he was crushed for our iniquities;
    the punishment that brought us peace was upon him,
    and by his wounds we are healed.
We all, like sheep, have gone astray,
    each of us has turned to his own way;
    and the Lord has laid on him the iniquity of us all.

Isaiah 53:4–6

Slaves, submit yourselves to your masters with all respect, not only to those who are good and considerate, but also to those who are harsh. For it is commendable if a man bears up under the pain of unjust suffering because he is conscious of God. But how is it to your credit if you receive a beating for doing wrong and endure it? But if you suffer for doing good and you endure it, this is commendable before God. To this you were called, because Christ suffered for you, leaving you an example, that you should follow in his steps.

1 Peter 2:18–21

The Gifts of Security and Comfort

If people have easily what they need and a lot of money in their coffers and guard against committing serious sins, they think everything is done. They enjoy what they have. They give alms from time to time. They do not reflect that their riches are not their own but given by the Lord so that they, as His stewards, may share their wealth among the poor, and that they must give a strict account for the time they keep a surplus in their coffers while delaying and putting off the poor who are suffering....

We must be content with little. We must not want as much as those who give a strict accounting, as any rich person will have to give, even though he may not have to do so here on earth. Always look for the poorest things ... if you don't, you will find yourself frustrated because God is not going to give you more, and you will be unhappy. Strive always to serve His Majesty in such a way that you do not eat the food of the poor without serving Him for it.

Teresa of Avila

How firm a foundation, ye saints of the Lord,
    is laid for your faith in His excellent Word!
What more can He say than to you He hath said—
    to you, who for refuge to Jesus have fled?

"When thru fiery trials thy pathway shall lie,
    My grace, all sufficient, shall be thy supply;
The flame shall not hurt thee—I only design
    Thy dross to consume and thy gold to refine."

"K"—in Rippon's Selection of Hymns, 1787

My people will live in peaceful dwelling places,
in secure homes, in undisturbed places of rest.

Isaiah 32:18

Burst into songs of joy together, you ruins of Jerusalem,
for the LORD has comforted his people, he has redeemed
    Jerusalem.
The LORD will lay bare his holy arm in the sight of all the nations,
and all the ends of the earth will see the salvation of our God.

Isaiah 52:9–10

The LORD will keep you from all harm—he will watch over
    your life;
the LORD will watch over your coming and going both now and
    forevermore.

Psalm 121:7–8

We have this hope as an anchor for the soul, firm and secure. It
enters the inner sanctuary behind the curtain, where Jesus, who
went before us, has entered on our behalf. He has become a high
priest forever, in the order of Melchizedek.

Hebrews 6:19–20

I will instruct you and teach you in the way you should go;
    I will counsel you and watch over you.

Psalm 32:8

PART FIVE

Seize the Day

*The difference between the impossible and the possible
lies in a man's determination.*

TOMMY LASORDA

Pursue Excellence and Wisdom

We could—some people do—believe that the sole purpose of life is to be comfortable. Gorge yourself, build a nice home, enjoy good food, have sex, live the good life. That's all there is. But the presence of suffering vastly complicates that lifestyle....

It's hard to believe the world is here just so I can party, when a third of its people go to bed starving each night. It's hard to believe the purpose of life is to feel good, when I see teenagers smashed on the freeway. If I try to escape toward hedonism, suffering and death lurk nearby, haunting me, reminding me of how hollow life would be if this world were all I'd ever know.

Sometimes murmuring, sometimes shouting, suffering is a "rumor of transcendence" that the entire human condition is out of whack. Something is wrong with a life of war and violence and human tragedy. He who wants to be satisfied with this world, who wants to believe the only purpose of life is enjoyment, must go around with cotton in his ears, for the megaphone of pain is a loud one.

Philip Yancey

Why is wisdom worth suffering for? Why is wisdom worth more than pleasure? Why is foolishness worse than pain? Because of what we are. We are not animals. We are human beings, with minds, souls, spirits, wills, and psyches. Wisdom is the food of our souls. Without it, we starve.

Peter Kreeft

Just as you excel in everything—in faith, in speech, in knowledge, in complete earnestness and in your love for us—see that you also excel in this grace of giving.... Finish the work, so that your eager willingness to do it may be matched by your completion of it, according to your means. For if the willingness is there, the gift is acceptable according to what one has, not according to what he does not have.

2 Corinthians 8:7, 11–12

Put to death, therefore, whatever belongs to your earthly nature: sexual immorality, impurity, lust, evil desires and greed, which is idolatry. Because of these, the wrath of God is coming. You used to walk in these ways, in the life you once lived. But now you must rid yourselves of all such things as these: anger, rage, malice, slander, and filthy language from your lips. Do not lie to each other, since you have taken off your old self with its practices and have put on the new self, which is being renewed in knowledge in the image of its Creator.... As God's chosen people, holy and dearly loved, clothe yourselves with compassion, kindness, humility, gentleness and patience. Bear with each other and forgive whatever grievances you may have against one another. Forgive as the Lord forgave you. And over all these virtues put on love, which binds them all together in perfect unity.

Colossians 3:5–10, 12–14

Wisdom, like an inheritance, is a good thing
and benefits those who see the sun.
Wisdom is a shelter as money is a shelter,
but the advantage of knowledge is this:
that wisdom preserves the life of its possessor.

Ecclesiastes 7:11–12

In the day of my trouble I will call to you, for you will
answer me.

Psalm 86:7

This is the day the LORD has made;
let us rejoice and be glad in it.

Psalm 118:24

This is what the LORD says:
"In the time of my favor I will answer you,
and in the day of salvation I will help you."

Isaiah 49:8

Praise the LORD.
Blessed is the man who fears the LORD,
who finds great delight in his commands.

Psalm 112:1

Therefore, my dear friends, as you have always obeyed—not only in my presence, but now much more in my absence—continue to work out your salvation with fear and trembling, for it is God who works in you to will and to act according to his good purpose. Do everything without complaining or arguing, so that you may become blameless and pure, children of God without fault in a crooked and depraved generation, in which you shine like stars in the universe as you hold out the word of life.

Philippians 2:12–16

Pursue Virtue

True virtue, as C. S. Lewis points out below, is not contingent on a prescribed set of actions—for those vary from culture to culture. The virtuous person is one whose intent in all things is to please God and to mirror, however imperfectly, his holiness and love. If we focus too much on individual actions, we fall either into relativism or legalism, neither of which glorify our heavenly Father.

While the rule of chastity is the same for all Christians at all times, the rule of propriety changes. A girl in the Pacific Islands wearing hardly any clothes and a Victorian lady completely covered in clothes might both be equally "modest," proper, or decent, according to the standards of their own society: and both, for all we could tell by their dress, might be equally chaste (or equally unchaste).

When people break the rule of propriety currently in their own time and place, if they do so to excite lust in themselves or in others, then they are offending against chastity. But if they break it out of ignorance or carelessness they are guilty only of bad manners. When, as often happens, they break it defiantly in order to shock or embarrass others, they are not necessarily being unchaste, but they are being uncharitable: for it is uncharitable to take pleasure in making other people uncomfortable.

C. S. Lewis

The reason so many of our youth can't distinguish between the real and the counterfeit, between truth and error, between what's moral and what's immoral, is because many parents have stopped measuring against the original. We all have been influenced by the cultural shift away from God as the center of all things. Our culture has rejected the Source of Truth and has tried to come up with its own ideas about right and wrong....

Too often, parents and other adults communicate to young people that their actions violate *the adult's* standard of decency, or ethics, or morality. That would be perfectly appropriate if absolute truth were defined by the individual. But it's not. It is God and God alone who determines absolute truth. Truth is objective because God exists outside ourselves; it is universal because God is above all; it is constant because God is eternal.

Josh McDowell

A wife of noble character, who can find?
She is worth far more than rubies.
Her husband has full confidence in her
and lacks nothing of value.
She brings him good, not harm, all the days of her life.

Proverbs 31:10–12

I urge, then, first of all, that requests, prayers, intercession and thanksgiving be made for everyone—for kings and all those in authority, that we may live peaceful and quiet lives in all godliness and holiness. This is good, and pleases God our Savior, who wants all men to be saved and to come to a knowledge of the truth.... I want men everywhere to lift up holy hands in prayer, without anger or disputing.

1 Timothy 2:1–4, 8

The fruit of the Spirit is love, joy, peace, patience, kindness, goodness, faithfulness, gentleness and self-control. Against such things there is no law.

Galatians 5:22–23

Blessed is the man
> who does not walk in the counsel of the
> > wicked
or stand in the way of sinners
> or sit in the seat of mockers.
But his delight is in the law of the LORD,
> and on his law he meditates day and
> > night.
He is like a tree planted by streams of water,
> which yields its fruit in season
and whose leaf does not wither.
> Whatever he does prospers.

Psalm 1:1–3

They who seek the L ORD will praise him —
    may your hearts live forever.

Psalm 22:26

I will always obey your law, for ever and ever.

Psalm 119:44

If we live, we live to the Lord; and if we die, we die to the Lord.
    So, whether we live or die, we belong to the Lord.

Romans 14:8

Find Fellowship

As children of God moving toward maturity, let's be committed to harmony, to a spirit of unity. Let's engage in a mutual interest in each other's lives. Let's develop friendships marked by affection, by "touchable love"—love that is genuine and demonstrative. Let's be kindhearted and compassionate. Let's exhibit humility of spirit and a mind that is concerned about others instead of ourselves. Finally, let's forgive, control our tongues, and pursue purity and peace.

Charles Swindoll

Friendship adds a brighter radiance to prosperity and lightens the burden of adversity by dividing and sharing it.

Cicero

We lose our friends, not by great decisions, but through small neglects.

Ancient Proverb

God has a special reason, a unique design in each friendship. He chose to surround your life with these certain treasured dear ones for good reason. These Christian friends are the ones with whom you will live for eternity, enjoying an even deeper dimension of friendship.

Joni Eareckson Tada

Small kindnesses make a difference—
they have echoes out of proportion to the effort they take.
"We do not do great things, only small things with great love...."

Sue Bender

Any good work, kindness or service I can render to any person
  or animal,
let me do it now. Let me not neglect or delay to do it,
for I will not pass this way again.

Old Quaker saying

Two are better then one, because they have a good return for their
  work:
If one falls down, his friend can help him up.
But pity the man who falls and has no one to help him up!
Also, if two lie down together, they will keep warm.
But how can one keep warm alone?
Though one may be overpowered, two can defend themselves.
A cord of three strands is not quickly broken.

Ecclesiastes 4:9–12

From one man God made every nation of men, that they should inhabit the whole earth; and he determined the times set for them and the exact places where they should live. God did this so that men would seek him and perhaps reach out for him and find him, though he is not far from each one of us. "For in him we live and move and have our being."

Acts 17:26–28

If you have any encouragement from being united with Christ, if any comfort from his love, if any fellowship with the Spirit, if any tenderness and compassion, then make my joy complete by being like-minded, having the same love, being one in spirit and purpose. Do nothing out of selfish ambition or vain conceit, but in humility consider others better than yourselves. Each of you should look not only to your own interests, but also to the interests of others.

Philippians 2:1–4

A man of many companions may come to ruin,
> but there is a friend who sticks closer than a brother.

Proverbs 18:24

Wounds from a friend can be trusted,
> but an enemy multiplies kisses.

Proverbs 27:6

Whoever loves his brother lives in the light, and there is nothing in him to make him stumble.

1 John 2:10

Do not think of yourself more highly than you ought, but rather think of yourself with sober judgment, in accordance with the measure of faith God has given you. Just as each of us has one body with many members, and these members do not all have the same function, so in Christ we who are many form one body, and each member belongs to all the others.

Romans 12:3–5

Serve Others in the Name of Jesus

Almost all of us rub shoulders every day with people who are seeking. They are looking for someone who will take the time and effort required to help them come to some solid conclusions about spiritual truth. You can see it in their eyes, can't you? Just look beneath the veneer, and you'll detect a longing for something deeper, something real and true and enduring.

Most of us grossly underestimate the effect we could have on people's eternities if we would take the time to schedule a breakfast or lunch with lost people in our sphere of influence. If we'd just make an appointment, and then take a risk in the conversation by clearly expressing the essence of what it means to know Christ personally, heaven only knows what might happen.

Have you given anybody the gift of time lately? When was the last time you hit the pause button on your overburdened schedule and just gave away an hour or two to a spiritual seeker?

Bill Hybels

It is hard for a young person with high ideals to learn that people cannot be hustled into the kingdom of God. Remember Christ's own descriptions of that kingdom: leaven and seed, things which work slowly and out of sight. We long for visible evidence of our effectiveness, and when it is not forthcoming, we may be tempted to conclude that our efforts never had anything to do with the kingdom.... [And yet,] to God nothing is finally lost.

All the scriptural metaphors about the death of the seed which falls into the ground, about losing one's life, about becoming least in the kingdom, about the world's passing away—all these go on to something unspeakably better and more glorious. Loss and death are only the preludes to life and gain.

Elisabeth Elliot

I am convinced that God's Holy Spirit orchestrates our lives to touch others—strangers, friends, work-related people, service-industry workers, and more—if we would just open up and be ourselves. How? Be free to be in love with Jesus in front of people. Be an ambassador through whom he can introduce himself. There is a world out there hungry and searching for Jesus and his love. Don't keep him to yourself.

Becky Tirabassi

Command those who are rich in this present world not to be arrogant nor to put their hope in wealth, which is so uncertain, but to put their hope in God, who richly provides us with everything for our enjoyment. Command them to do good, to be rich in good deeds, and to be generous and willing to share. In this way they will lay up treasure for themselves as a firm foundation for the coming age, so that they may take hold of the life that is truly life.

1 Timothy 6:17–19

Seek Personal Growth

What if you and I were videotaped for at least a week—every day, all day—at home, at work, at play—and then the video played back for our church, family, friends, anyone who looks up to us? Would we talk and act differently? Would we live differently? Does the very thought of a daily videotape send shivers up your spine? It would show so much about how we live and who we are living for. The truth is that God *is* watching. He *is* aware. Not with a gigantic teaching stick in one hand and a check-off list in the other, but with eyes that see to our very core—eyes desiring that we live in the riches of his grace so that we may be able to eat of the good fruit that comes from a life rooted in love. Now *that* is abundant life.

Kathy Troccoli

We have a tendency to look for wonder in our experience, and we mistake heroic actions for real heroes. It's one thing to go through a crisis grandly, yet quite another to go through every day glorifying God when there is no witness, no limelight, and no one paying even the remotest attention to us.... If you are properly devoted to Jesus Christ, you have reached the lofty height where no one would ever notice you personally. All that is noticed is the power of God coming through you all the time.

Oswald Chambers

Believe it or not, it's possible to overdose on expressing compassion. I know some people in our church who early in their Christian lives got so fired up that they sort of unzipped their chests and offered their hearts to every needy person who came their way. They were so overwhelmed by God's grace that they wanted to be conduits of His love to every troubled person they could find. And so they gave and gave; in fact, they gave so excessively they were ready to give out....

Unfortunately, many people never learned that caring for others has to be meticulously balanced with caring for yourself. This is how to prevent burn-out in the process of giving compassion, and it's a pattern that Jesus often demonstrated. He gave out enormous amounts of care, but then on a regular basis He said, in effect, "Enough is enough. Now I'm going to the mountain to pray and be alone, where I can rest and recuperate."

Bill Hybels

It was Christ who gave some to be apostles, some to be prophets, some to be evangelists, and some to be pastors and teachers, to prepare God's people for works of service, so that the body of Christ may be built up until we all reach unity in the faith and in the knowledge of the Son of God and become mature, attaining to the whole measure of the fullness of Christ. Then we will no longer be infants, tossed back and forth by the waves, and blown here and there by every wind of teaching and by the cunning and craftiness of men in their deceitful scheming. Instead, speaking the truth in love, we will in all things grow up into him who is the Head, that is, Christ. From him the whole body, joined and held together by every supporting ligament, grows and builds itself up in love, as each part does its work.

Ephesians 4:11–16

Rid yourselves of all malice and all deceit, hypocrisy, envy, and slander of every kind. Like newborn babes, crave pure spiritual milk, so that by it you may grow up in your salvation, now that you have tasted that the Lord is good.

1 Peter 2:1–3

I pray that out of his glorious riches the Father may strengthen you with power through his Spirit in your inner being, so that Christ may dwell in your hearts through faith. And I pray that you, being rooted and established in love, may have power, together with all the saints, to grasp how wide and long and high and deep is the love of Christ, and to know this love that surpasses knowledge—that you may be filled to the measure of all the fullness of God.

Ephesians 3:16–19

But grow in the grace and knowledge of our Lord and Savior Jesus Christ. To him be glory both now and forever! Amen.

2 Peter 3:18

I planted the seed, Apollos watered it, but God made it grow.

1 Corinthians 3:6

Therefore I tell you, whatever you ask for in prayer, believe that you have received it, and it will be yours.

Mark 11:24

Be joyful in hope, patient in affliction, faithful in prayer.

Romans 12:12

Learn Discipline

The Christian life is a continual process of growth.
Sometimes the most valuable lessons and the strongest
"growth spurts" come when we persevere in our faith
through the most unlikely circumstances.

That summer's experience selling Fuller brushes taught me a lot about myself, about human nature, and about communicating a message to people even if I had to talk my way in and out of all kinds of situations. I did not win any awards or honors from the company, but in the poorer areas that I was assigned to, I had done well enough to earn sometimes as much as $50 or $75 in a week, almost a fortune then for a teenager. And being away from my parents, learning to make my own way, gave me self-confidence.

I learned a lot about prayer too. I developed a practice of praying about every call as I walked up to the door, asking God to give me an opportunity to witness for Christ. At times I was somewhat headstrong about this, not really sensitive to the leading of the Holy Spirit. [My mentor] Albert got complaints from some of our customers that I was trying to give them a hard sell about Christ as much as Fuller brushes. He rightly cautioned me to be more discerning.

Billy Graham

If there is a God, and if that God is righteous, then no creature under His righteous authority ever has the right to do wrong.

Here the righteousness of God explodes on the scene of human ethical behavior. There is nothing remote or abstract about the righteousness of God. It has everything to do with what we do. His righteousness is the ultimate standard of our behavior, of our laws, and of our lives.

R. C. Sproul

I used to think discipline and self-control was a natural by-product of a supernatural holiness and revival. But now I see that lack of self-discipline is keeping my holiness (which I already have in Jesus) from controlling my life and coming to the surface. This is a brand-new view, and I believe I've isolated the enemy's greatest stronghold in my life at this time....

Discipline is not holiness—nor the way to holiness—it just helps you to maintain it.

Keith Green

My son, do not despise the LORD's discipline
and do not resent his rebuke,
because the LORD disciplines those he loves,
as a father the son he delights in.

Proverbs 3:11–12

If any of you lacks wisdom, he should ask God, who gives generously to all without finding fault, and it will be given to him. But
when he asks, he must believe and not doubt, because he who
doubts is like a wave of the sea, blown and tossed by the wind.
That man should not think he will receive anything from the
Lord; he is a double-minded man, unstable in all he does....
Blessed is the man who perseveres under trial, because when he
has stood the test, he will receive the crown of life that God has
promised to those who love him.

James 1:5–8, 12

Create in me a pure heart, O God, and renew a steadfast spirit
within me.

Psalm 51:10

In your anger do not sin;
    when you are on your beds,
    search your hearts and be silent.

Psalm 4:4

Search me, O God, and know my heart;
    test me and know my anxious thoughts.

Psalm 139:23

Pay attention and listen to the sayings of the wise;
    apply your heart to what I teach,
for it is pleasing when you keep them in your heart
    and have all of them ready on your lips.

Proverbs 22:17, 18

Do not be deceived: God cannot be mocked. A man reaps what he sows. The one who sows to please his sinful nature, from that nature will reap destruction; the one who sows to please the Spirit, from the Spirit will reap eternal life. Let us not become weary in doing good, for at the proper time we will reap a harvest if we do not give up. Therefore, as we have opportunity, let us do good to all people, especially to those who belong to the family of believers.

Galatians 6:7–10

Live Purposefully

A person can give his life to no greater good than Christ Himself. God formed us for Himself. We can only find our fulfillment in Him.

To devote ourselves to anything less or anyone else is to actually deprive both ourselves and Him of His highest purposes for us. It is to settle for less than His greatest aspirations for us. It is to come down to the end of our brief lives, only to discover in dismay that in failing to truly love Him, we have failed altogether.

W. Phillip Keller

C.S. Lewis said, "Aim at heaven and you get earth thrown in. Aim at earth and you get neither." When a Christian realizes his citizenship is in heaven, he begins acting as a responsible citizen of earth. He invests wisely in relationships because he knows they're eternal. His conversations, goals, and motives become pure and honest because he realizes these will have a bearing on his everlasting reward. He gives generously of time, money, and talent because he's laying up treasures for eternity. He spreads the good news of Christ because he loves to fill heaven's ranks with his friends and neighbors. All this serves the pilgrim not only in heaven, but on earth; for it serves everyone around him.

Joni Eareckson Tada

For God, who said, "Let light shine out of darkness," made his light shine in our hearts to give us the light of the knowledge of the glory of God in the face of Christ. But we have this treasure in jars of clay to show that this all-surpassing power is from God and not from us. We are hard pressed on every side, but not crushed; perplexed, but not in despair; persecuted, but not abandoned; struck down, but not destroyed. We always carry around in our body the death of Jesus, so that the life of Jesus may also be revealed in our body. For we who are alive are always being given over to death for Jesus' sake, so that his life may be revealed in our mortal body. So then, death is at work in us, but life is at work in you.

2 Corinthians 4:6–12

You are the salt of the earth. But if the salt loses its saltiness, how can it be made salty again? It is no longer good for anything, except to be thrown out and trampled…. You are the light of the world. A city on a hill cannot be hidden. Neither do people light a lamp and put it under a bowl. Instead they put it on its stand, and it gives light to everyone in the house. In the same way, let your light shine before men, that they may see your good deeds and praise your Father in heaven.

Matthew 5:13–16

Fight the good fight of the faith. Take hold of the eternal life to which you were called when you made your good confession in the presence of many witnesses. In the sight of God … keep this command without spot or blame until the appearing of our Lord Jesus Christ, which God will bring about in his own time—God, the blessed and only Ruler, the King of kings and Lord of lords, who alone is immortal and who lives in unapproachable light, whom no one has seen or can see. To him be honor and might forever. Amen.

1 Timothy 6:12–16

Selections taken from:

Sue Bender, *Everyday Sacred* (San Francisco, CA: HarperCollins, 1995).

William Bennett, *The Book of Virtues* (New York, NY: Simon & Schuster, 1993).

Paul E. Billheimer, *Don't Waste Your Sorrows* (Minneapolis, MN: Bethany, 1977).

Dr. Paul Brand, *Fearfully and Wonderfully Made* (Grand Rapids, MI: Zondervan, 1987).

Bob Briner, *Roaring Lambs* (Grand Rapids, MI: Zondervan, 1993).

Julia Cameron, *The Artist's Way* (New York, NY: Putnam Books, 1992).

Oswald Chambers, *My Utmost for His Highest*, special updated edition, James Reimann, ed. (Grand Rapids, MI: Discovery House, 1995).

Margaret Clarkson, *Grace Grows Best in Winter* (Grand Rapids, MI: Eerdmans, 1984).

Lloyd Cory (comp.), *Quote-Unquote* (Wheaton, IL: SP Publications, Victor Books, 1977).

L. B. Cowman, *Streams in the Desert* (Grand Rapids, MI: Zondervan, 1996).

Francis de Sales, *Thy Will Be Done* (Manchester, NH: Sophia Press, 1995).

Dave and Jan Dravecky, *Do Not Lose Heart* (Grand Rapids, MI: Zondervan, 1998).

Elisabeth Elliot, *A Chance To Die* (Old Tappan, NJ: Revell, 1987).

Elisabeth Elliot, *Passion and Purity* (Old Tappan, NJ: Revell, 1984).

Debra Evans, *Women of Character* (Grand Rapids, MI: Zondervan, 1996).

John Fischer, *True Believers Don't Ask Why* (Minneapolis, MN: Bethany, 1989).

Billy Graham, *Hope for the Troubled Heart* (Nashville, TN: Word, 1991).

Billy Graham. *Just As I Am* (New York, NY: HarperCollins Publishers, 1997).

Keith Green, *No Compromise* (Chatsworth, CA: Sparrow, 1989).

Bill Hybels, *Becoming a Contagious Christian* (Grand Rapids, MI: Zondervan, 1996).

Phillip Keller. *A Layman Looks at the Love of God* (Minneapolis, MN: Bethany, 1984).

Peter Kreeft, *Making Sense Out of Suffering* (Ann Arbor, MI: Servant, 1986).

C. S. Lewis, *Mere Christianity* (New York, NY: Macmillan, 1952).

C. S. Lewis, *The Four Loves* (Orlando, FL: Harcourt Brace, 1988).

Josh McDowell and Bob Hostetler, *Right From Wrong* (Dallas, TX: Word, 1994).

Vernon McLellan, *Timeless Treasures* (Nashville, TN: Thomas Nelson, 1992).

Kathleen Norris, *Amazing Grace* (New York, NY: Riverhead Books, 1998).

Lloyd Ogilvie, *A Future and a Hope* (Nashville, TN: Word, 1988).

Constance and Daniel Pollack (ed.), *The Book of Uncommon Prayer* (Dallas, TX: Word, 1996).

Stacy & Paula Rinehart, *Choices* (Colorado Springs, CO: Navpress, 1982).

Edith Schaeffer, *The Tapestry* (Waco, TX: Word, 1981).

Dutch Sheets, *Intercessory Prayer: How God Can Use Your Prayer to Move Heaven and Earth* (Ventura, CA: Regal, 1996).

Quin Sherrer, *Miracles Happen When You Pray* (Grand Rapids, MI: Zondervan, 1997).

R. C. Sproul, *The Character of God* (Ann Arbor, MI: Servant, 1995).

R. C. Sproul, "Catholicism" *Christianity Today,* 1/8/96.

Charles H. Spurgeon, *Morning and Evening* (Nashville, TN: Thomas Nelson, 1994) .

Charles R. Swindoll, *Hope Again* (Dallas, TX: Word, 1996).

Joni Eareckson Tada, *Diamonds in the Dust* (Grand Rapids, MI: Zondervan, 1993).

Joni Eareckson Tada, *Heaven: Your Real Home* (Grand Rapids, MI: Zondervan, 1995).

Mother Teresa, *In My Own Words* (Ligouri, MO: Ligouri, 1996).

Teresa of Avila, *The Interior Castle: The Collected Works of St. Teresa of Avila,* Vol. 2 (Washington, D.C.: ICS Publications, 1980).

Becky Tirabassi, *Wild Things Happen When I Pray* (Grand Rapids, MI: Zondervan, 1993).

Kathy Troccoli, *My Life Is in Your Hands* (Grand Rapids, MI: Zondervan, 1997).

Sheldon Vanauken, *Under the Mercy* (San Francisco, CA: Ignatius, 1988).

Sheila Walsh, *Honestly* (Grand Rapids, MI: Zondervan, 1996).

Neil Clark Warren, *Finding Contentment* (Nashville, TN: Thomas Nelson, 1997).

Where Only Love Can Go (Notre Dame, IN: Ave Maria, 1996).

Philip Yancey, *The Jesus They Never Knew* (Grand Rapids, MI: Zondervan, 1995).

Philip Yancey, *Where Is God When It Hurts?* (Grand Rapids, MI: Zondervan, 1990, 1997).